SKATEBOARDING BASICS: YOUR BEGINNERS GUIDE

Mike Topkin

D0001403

Skateboarding Basics: Your Beginners Guide

ISBN-13: 978-1481119504
ISBN-10: 1481119508

Copyright Notice

For skateboarders everywhere...

Contents

No one can say for sure when the sport of skateboarding was officially developed, but it's generally believed to have begun sometime in the late 1940s or early 1950s.

And just as the exact time of development isn't known, the identity of the person who made the very first skateboard also isn't known.

The generally accepted theory is that California surfers came up with the sport as a way of surfing on land, when the ocean waves were too flat for them to surf on.

These surfers used wooden boxes and boards to which roller skate wheels were attached.

Over time, the boxes were replaced by planks, until sporting goods manufacturers came up with pressed wooden decks that more closely resembled the skateboards commonly seen today.

Due to the fact that the sport was originally seen as an alternative to surfing, it was originally known as Sidewalk Surfing.

As the sport became more and more popular, manufacturers started creating skateboards that looked like small surfboards on wheels.

The sport's popularity even led to the publication of a national magazine called the Skateboarder Magazine.

The year 1965 saw the very first international skateboarding championship broadcast on national TV. The sales figures of skateboard manufacturers during the early part of this decade also made the sport's growing popularity very obvious.

This popularity, however, dropped in 1966 along with the sales figures.

The Skateboarder Magazine even stopped publication in that same year.

The popularity of skateboarding only began to pick up once again in the 1970s, when Frank Nasworthy started developing wheels made of polyurethane and then called it "the Cadillac."

Manufacturers also worked on improving traction and performance at that time.

As a result, skateboards became more manoeuvrable and skateboarders started having more control over their boards.

As the sport continued to grow in popularity, manufacturers began experimenting with materials like aluminium and fibreglass.

Skateboarders also started experimenting with tricks as the handling of their skateboards improved.

In 1976, California experienced a drought that emptied most of their favourite swimming pools.

Enterprising individuals then made vertical walls from these pools, which resulted in the birth of skateboarding.

This gave skateboarders the opportunity to skate even faster and perform even more dangerous tricks like slash grinds and backside airs.

The drawback was that insurance costs increased and many skate parks had to close down. This led skateboarders to making their own ramps.

Even more vert tricks were invented in the 1980s, but street skating still grew in popularity because a majority of skateboarders didn't have access to vert ramps and couldn't afford to make their own ramps.

These days, the sport is dominated by street skaters and most skateboards are 30-32 inches long and 7.5-8 inches wide.

Skateboard wheels are now usually made of extremely hard polyurethane. The boards are also lighter and more manageable, owing to smaller wheels.

Although the styles of skateboards evolved dramatically since the 1970s, the form adopted in the 1980s have become standard and mostly remained constant since the 1990s.

Popularity of Skateboarding

Over the last fifty years or so, no other cultural or sporting revolution has had the same success or impact skateboarding has had.

Its modest beginnings as an alternative sport to surfing in California have led skateboarding all the way to becoming a mainstream activity.

In fact, the sport has exploded in popularity unlike anything else either before or after its invention.

But, when you take the time to think seriously about it, it's not really that surprising why skateboarding enjoyed a massive popularity and is expected to continue doing so.

Although it requires a great deal of skill, excellent balance, and physical dexterity in order for you to achieve the skateboarding levels of professionals like Tony Hawk, the good thing about skateboarding is that it doesn't involve too much cost.

And if you're taking up the sport solely for recreational purposes, then it won't involve too much of a challenge either.

All that's really needed to start with is for you to buy a skateboard, which is a lot less expensive than the equipment required in other sporting activities.

You'd also do well to buy a helmet as well as elbow and knee pads.

Other than that, there's hardly anything else you need to buy for learning how to skateboard.

Many people may not look at it this way, but skateboarding is actually an excellent form of exercise and a great way for you to keep in shape.

This may even be one of the reasons why it has remained popular over the years. Those who've tried it appreciate the fact that the constant balancing and shifting of your position and body weight provides a number of physical benefits.

This shifting and balancing is necessary for the safe and proper execution of your skateboarding tricks.

And while you may not immediately see the health and physical benefits provided by the sport, you surely won't miss them over time.

As your skills the sport increase, you'll surely notice that your body has also become a lot more balanced and coordinated.

Other than that, skateboarding has also gained popularity because of the fact that it is an excellent way of declaring your independence and standing out from the crowd.

Try to observe skateboarders for some time and you'll notice how they seem to lead such carefree lives.

This doesn't necessarily mean they don't take life seriously; it simply means they've developed the patience, hearty attitude, and willingness to get up immediately after a fall that's necessary to succeed in the sport.

When you come to think about it, these attributes are necessary for succeeding in life as well.

Being engaged in skateboarding also provides you with access to locations you otherwise would never even think of visiting.

And riding on a skateboard allows you to traverse areas that may not be that accessible to other modes of transport.

Furthermore, if you constantly practice and hone whatever skateboarding skills you have, then you'll surely achieve the highest levels of confidence and control.

In time, you'll be amazed at the tricks you're able to perform with your board.

What Makes
Skateboarding Popular

If you're a fan of the X Games, then you know that skateboarding is among these games' most popular sports.

Held on an annual basis, the X Games focus mainly on activities categorized as extreme action sports.

The sport of skateboarding, in particular, has become all the rage among younger athletes.

The skills, speed, and creativity that goes into skateboarding tricks definitely make it highly interesting and challenging.

Skateboarding enthusiasts agree that the sport is all about the passion, the speed, and the thrill.

If you're wondering why such a dangerous sport has become so popular, here are just a few reasons:

1. Health Benefits

Like any other sporting activity, skateboarding offers a number of health benefits.

People lead such sedentary lifestyles these days that cases of obesity and other diseases have risen in number among younger individuals.

Skateboarding effectively increases your fitness level while helping you lose weight and get in shape at the same time.

Among other things, it enhances your cardiovascular health and aids in improving your physical appearance.

So, if you're looking for a sporting activity that's entertaining and promotes fitness at the same time, then skateboarding is indeed the right sport for you.

2. Social Benefits

Skateboarding is known to be an excellent way of making new friends and bonding with old ones.

Once you start learning the sport, you're bound to come into contact with others who are also just starting out as well as skateboarders who've been engaged in the sport for years.

In time, you may even want to invite your friends to get into the sport as well.

Not only does this effectively increase your circle of friends, but it also gives you an excellent opportunity for learning new tricks and valuable tips for enhancing your skills in the sport.

You could even meet a training partner who can help motivate you towards enhancing your overall performance.

3. Athletic Benefits

Skateboarding isn't just a recreational sport anymore. In fact, a lot of people have taken up the sport professionally.

Of course, becoming a professional skateboarder requires regular practice and a proper training schedule.

It also requires dedication, patience, and a real passion for the sport.

It's a good idea to hire a professional trainer who can instruct you in the fundamentals of the sport and guide you towards becoming an advanced skateboarder.

Take note that just like in any other sport, it's essential to master the basics of skateboarding before you even think about attempting complicated tricks and stunts.

In time, your training should lead you towards becoming a professional skateboarder and winning major skateboarding events.

4. Economical Benefits

One of the best things about skateboarding is that it isn't as expensive as other sports. The only things you need to invest in for starters are your skateboard, a helmet, elbow pads, and knee pads.

As your skills improve, you may want to buy specially-designed skateboarding shoes and other specialized gear as well.

But, even with the most advanced skateboarding gear, the sport is still a lot less expensive than other sporting activities.

Now that you know what benefits the sport of skateboarding has to offer, it should be easier to understand why this has become very popular over the years and why it's a good idea for you to take up the sport as well.

Protective Gear for Skateboarding

Skateboarding is an exciting sport enjoyed by people of all ages. Take note, however, that your skateboarding adventure could become very painful unless you wear the proper gear.

The sport involves a lot of tricks and stunts, which is why it can be a little dangerous to engage in if you're not wearing protective gear.

To make sure you have complete protective gear when you go skateboarding, it's advisable to check from your head downwards.

Here are the most important items you should be wearing when you go "surfing the sidewalk."

Head and Face

A skateboarding helmet is, of course, among the essential items that need to be included in your protective gear.

Needless to say, it keeps your head from getting as easily cracked as an egg in case you fall.

When you go shopping for a skateboarding helmet, be sure to choose one that's just right for your size, age, and preferences.

Other than your head, you also need protection for your eyes when you skateboard. Protective sunglasses are your best option towards this end.

Many skateboarders take their eyes for granted and wear protective glasses only when the sun is shining particularly bright.

But, it's never a good idea to take unnecessary risks where your eyes are concerned, so it's best to wear sunglasses every time you skate.

In the same way, it's advisable to wear a mouth guard although this protective item is generally considered optional.

Elbows and Wrists

Some people don't like wearing elbow pads when they go skateboarding. If you're like these people, then wearing a full-sleeved shirt is a good option for you.

Take note, though, that even a full-sleeved shirt can't offer the same amount of protection you can get from elbow pads.

Wrist injury is another thing you should protect yourself against when you engage in the sport of skateboarding.

Among the best ways to reduce the risk for such injuries is to wear a pair of wrist guards. You may really like it, but it's always smart to stay safe.

Knees

As a beginner in the sport, there's a good chance that you'll fall on your knees a number of times.

That will surely hurt a lot and may even force you to stay away from skating for some time.

If you don't want that to happen, then be sure to protect your knees when you skateboard.

The best way to do this is to wear a pair of knee pads of excellent quality.

If you can't afford to buy a good pair of knee pads just yet or don't have time to shop for them, then it's best to wear jeans for protection.

Ankles and Feet

You also need to protect your ankles and feet, of course. For ankle protection, you have the option to wear ankle braces. However, these can actually increase the risk for upper leg injury.

For this reason, you should only wear ankle braces if you've previously suffered from ankle problems.

Otherwise, you could forego the braces and focus on getting the right pair of skateboarding shoes instead. It's not advisable to go skateboarding in regular running shoes.

Instead, you should visit your local skateboarding goods store and look for specially-designed skateboarding shoes to protect both your ankles and your feet.

Choosing The Right Shoes

When you go out to shop for a pair of skateboarding shoes, you'll have to take a number of things into consideration.

After all, you wouldn't want to go all-out on your first day of learning how to skateboard only to have your shoes falling apart at the end of the day, right?

The right fit and comfort are, of course, among the most important thing for you to judge a pair of shoes by.

Other than these, there are a number of other features you'd do well to note in skateboarding shoes.

Skateboarding is a sport that's participated in not only by boys, but by girls as well. In fact, one of the most popular brands of skateboarding shoes is mostly targeted towards female skaters.

Although many people criticize these shoes because of their trademark laces, they're known to be very durable and long-lasting, which is perhaps their strongest point.

The good thing about these shoes is that their manufacturer is part of the group that's actively working on biomechanical skate shoes research, so you're definitely assured of the quality of the shoes.

And because each brand has its own quirks, anyway, the manufacturer has decided to keep their laces.

Regardless of what brand of skateboarding shoes you buy, though, you'll eventually wear them out in time.

When the soles start to fall off, you may want to extend the life of your shoes by using a special kind of rubber cement that's generally known as shoe goo.

In fact, this product can serve as a very effective preventive measure against any damage that may be caused by the normally abrasive surface of the commonly used grip tape.

The value of this can be felt even more if you choose to buy discount brand shoes, as these shoes aren't as sturdy as other brands.

If you find yourself with damaged skateboard shoes and shoe goo isn't on hand, duct tape could work in a pinch.

When you're shopping for skateboarding shoes, be sure to compare durability options such as action leather and toe cap plastic.

Some brands of skateboarding shoes may have become so popular that they're largely criticized for becoming too mainstream.

Even so, you may still find some of these shoes highly effective and ideal for skateboarding. If you believe that you could be spending most of your skateboarding time in conditions that aren't ideal, then you may want to invest in waterproof shoes.

You'd also do well to find shoes equipped with extra tread, which provides you with more grip. When things get a bit wet, you can be sure of still being in control.

You may also want to consider getting your shoes from a private reserve line. These shoes typically have better construction and you may appreciate the art featured on their insoles.

Some skateboarders also prefer shoes that have a worn-in appearance even when bought brand-new.

The design of shoes you choose primarily depends on your preferences as long as you make sure they don't sacrifice durability for style.

Choosing a Skateboard

Skateboarding is a tough and challenging sport. It requires a lot of dedication and constant practice to become an excellent skateboarder.

Other than that, you also need to choose the right skateboard that suits your personal skating style.

Take note that there are several different ways for you to put together a skateboarding, mixing and matching the different parts.

Decks, trucks, wheels, and bearings are the most basic parts you'll have to put together if you want to engage in the sport.

You should also bear in mind that skateboarding can be a dangerous sport, which makes it extremely important to take the necessary precautions.

When you select a deck for your board, remember that you need to do more than just choose the design.

There are several components you'll have to consider.

Among the first of these components is the deck's size. Skateboard decks often range in size from 29 inches and below or 32.4 inches and more.

The best way to choose the right deck size is to base it on your own height.

The taller you are, the longer your skateboard deck should be.

The width of a deck also differs and the right one depends on the size of your own feet.

If you have relatively wide feet, then your deck should be wider as well.

Another thing you need to choose carefully when you build your skateboard is the type of wheels.

You'll be surprised at how much difference a set of wheels can make in your performance. There are different sizes for skateboard wheels.

The bigger your wheels are, the faster your board will roll. If you like using ramps more than cruising on the streets, then larger wheels are definitely a good option for you.

However, if you're the stationary type of skateboarder, then you'd do well to choose smaller wheels.

Take note as well that harder wheels generally offer more stability whereas softer wheels provide better grip.

Your choice of wheels will depend largely on the type of skateboarding you choose to engage in.

Bearings are also important considerations because bad bearings make it more difficult for you to ride and will more likely result in a bumpy ride.

Spin the wheel of a skateboard to see how long it spins.

The longer it keeps on spinning, the better its bearings are. Bearings are typically rated from 1 to 9.

A higher number signifies more precision, but less strength. Take note that most skateboarders go for bearings rated 3 to 5.

You also have to choose your trucks correctly. These are the things that connect your wheels to the deck. A truck's width should match that of the deck. Specifically, it should be at least a fourth of the deck size.

In choosing the truck's height, you should once again consider the type of skateboarding you'll be engaged in.

Higher trucks are best for achieving more speed while lower trucks are best for stationary skateboarding.

Trucks typically have a bushing. Stiffer bushings are ideal for stationary skateboarding while softer bushings are best for making quick turns.

Bearing all these tips in mind, you should now be in a better position to choose the best skateboard that suits your skateboarding style.

Remember to always consider your safety first.

Choosing
Skateboard Wheels

Just as the tyres of your car can greatly influence the way it moves along the road, the wheels of a skateboard also largely determines the amount of stability and enjoyment a rider gets.

The good thing is that as long as you know exactly what to look for in skateboard wheels, you'll be sure to find the right kind of wheels that'll cater to your preferences and needs.

Riding Style

One of the most important considerations when you're choosing wheels for your skateboard is your regular riding style.

That's because the size of wheel you need is largely influenced by your style of riding.

For example, if you're fond of street skateboarding and doing tricks close to the ground, then the best option for you would be smaller wheels.

They give you a much lower centre of gravity, which makes the board a lot easier to manoeuvre and more secure.

On the other hand, if your preference is more for the longboard style, then you'll likely need bigger wheels.

These wheels provide you with more speed and allow you to cover longer distances.

Skateboarders usually use longboards for commuting across towns with a number of sidewalks, so it definitely makes sense to get larger wheels.

These wheels are also ideal if you normally perform skateboarding tricks on ramps, which typically require high speeds for safe execution.

Most skateboard wheels these days are made of polyurethane, which is quite a durable material.

Hardness

It's also a good idea to note just how hard the wheels are. The degree of hardness in skateboard wheels is also known as durometer.

The general rule is that harder wheels provide more speed whereas softer wheels provide better traction over a variety of terrain.

You'll therefore have to evaluate what characteristic you deem more important by considering the kind of environment and conditions in which you usually ride.

To make your skateboard relatively versatile, you'd do well to choose wheels that have a durometer of about 95A to 100A, as this range typically has the best features for multitasking skateboarders.

It generally offers a smooth ride along with excellent grip on various surfaces.

Colours

It can be quite surprising and a bit difficult to believe, but experts say the colour of your skateboard wheels actually affect their toughness.

Translucent wheels are said to be the most durable and the least prone to develop flat areas, since they don't have dyes that interfere with the amount of polyurethane in the formulation.

Polyurethane is what gives the wheels their strength, so the more there is in the wheels, the stronger the wheels are expected to be.

Your choice of colour will therefore be a decision between substance and style. The good thing is that skateboard wheels are typically easy to replace.

Keeping the above tips in mind, it should now be much easier for you to shop for the right skateboard wheels that serve your purposes and meet your needs best.

Start putting your board together now and take your skateboarding skills to an entirely new level.

Putting Your
Skateboard Together

The task of putting together a skateboard can become a bit overwhelming for a first timer, but just by following some simple steps, you should be able to complete the process without too much hassle.

You can start by clearing out the place where you plan to work. Arrange all the skateboard parts you have on the floor so you can check to make sure everything's complete and in good condition.

Bear in mind that you need four wheels, eight nuts, bolts, and bearings, one deck and grip sheet, and one pair of trucks.

When everything's in place, get the necessary tools, which include a knife, a file, a socket wrench, and a screwdriver or Allen wrench, depending on your bolts.

Now, you're ready to start the actual process of putting your skateboard together. Here's how:

1. Place your deck face-down on the floor. Peel off the grip sheet's backing and then stick it such that the board is completely covered. Don't worry if the sheet is a bit crooked, as long as it covers the board entirely, as you can easily trim it later.

2. Run the file around the board's outline so as to create a line, which makes it easier to trim off any excess grip sheet. Trim the edges carefully with the knife and then poke holes with the screwdriver through the grip where you'll be installing the hardware.

3. Install the trucks. Be sure to do this correctly because the manner in which the trucks are installed can affect the handling of your skateboard. Put the bolts through the prepared holes and then place the trucks on the bolts.

   When you tighten the bolts, make sure the kingpin – the bolt holding everything together – is faced inwards. When you're done installing the trucks, the two kingpins should be faced towards each other.

4. Press two bearing into each wheel. Hold the board on its side and then remove the nut from its axle. Place a bearing on the axle and then slide a wheel on. Press down on the wheel such that the bearing pops into place.

   Put another bearing into the wheel and repeat the process with the three other wheels. Replace the nut when all bearings in the four wheels are in place.

5. Attach the wheels to the board using the wrench. Be sure to tighten the wheels so they don't cause accidents by falling off. When all wheels are in place, test them as well as the trucks to ensure that they're working perfectly.

   If you notice even the slightest problem with how the wheels or trucks work, make the necessary adjustment before going for a test ride. If everything seems to work smoothly, then you can go ahead and test you skateboard.

So, you see, putting together your skateboard isn't really all that complicated.

While the thought of it may seem overwhelming at first, it's really quite easy when you get right down to it.

Just follow the simple instructions here and you be on your way to enjoying this exciting sport!

Balancing on Your Skateboard

As a beginner in the sport of skateboarding, among the very first things you should learn, of course, is the skill of balancing on your skateboard.

That may sound easy enough to do, but once you try it, you'll soon realize that it's actually not as easy as it seems.

And you'll also understand why this is the first thing you need to master.

After all, how can you ride your board successfully and execute skateboarding tricks if you can't even balance yourself on the board?

Here's how to successfully achieve balance on a skateboard:

1. Determine Your Stance

If you go right ahead and jump onto your skateboard when you don't have any background in the sport, you'll likely wobble a bit at best and end up cating dirt at worst.

The reason why many people struggle with balancing on a skateboard is that they don't know their own stance.

Learning your stance is therefore the necessary first step towards achieving balance.

The regular stance is when you have your left foot forward and you're facing towards the right.

If you skate facing the left and with your right foot forward, then you have the goofy stance. Try doing both to determine which feels more natural.

2. Get on the Board

As soon as you've determined your skateboarding stance, you should be ready to get on your board and give balancing a try.

Try to stand up straight and remember to keep your weight on both feet as you balance on the board.

Spread your legs as far as you can while still being comfortable and then slightly bend your knees so as to lower the centre of gravity as you find your balance.

You may also use your arms when trying to gain balance on the skateboard.

3. Practice

Once you've gotten the basics of balancing on a skateboard down, all that remains for you to do is to keep practicing.

As with anything else, practice indeed makes perfect for balancing on a skateboard.

Be sure to practice balancing while you're standing still, while you're rolling, and while you're turning.

When you start rolling, be sure not to go too fast at first.

Remember that your goal at this point is to learn how to balance and not how to ride. The riding part will come later.

Don't get too excited, as that could increase your risk of getting injured.

When you've finally mastered the skill of balancing on your skateboard while standing, rolling, and turning, then you're finally ready to start learning how to actually ride your board.

This time, you should start wearing the necessary protective gear each time you go out to practice.

Even when you're just practicing the basics, it's still important to put safety above all other considerations.

Other than always wearing protective gear, you should also practice in a safe location at all times.

If possible, practice in a spot that isn't too crowded so you can avoid hurting yourself and others in the process.

How to Grip a Skateboard

The fact that you're reading this only means you're interested in getting into the sport of skateboarding, among the most important steps to which is learning how to grip your board.

Here are a few simple steps that can guide you towards mastering the task of gripping your skateboard:

1. Prepare all the things you will need for the task. These things include your board, the grip tape, a sharp razor blade, a file, and a screwdriver. You'd also do well to have a pencil on hand or anything you can use to poke the holes of your skateboard with. Arrange these things on a flat surface that doesn't have any clutter. The floor or any table that doesn't wobble should suffice.

2. Place your board on the table or floor with the side featuring the graphics facing down. Grab the grip tape and then peel off its back paper. Attach the grip tape firmly onto your skateboard, making sure it's taped evenly and smoothly. Push down firmly on it to make sure it doesn't fly off.

3. Grab the file or anything you may have prepared to serve as a file and then file the tape firmly onto your skateboard's edges. You'll know that you've done this correctly if your see the grip tape apparently starting to change its colour. To be specific, the tape should start appearing white. This would indicate that the grip tape is already secure against the edges of the board.

4. Pick up the razor blade and then slice off any excess grip tape that may be protruding on the edges of the skateboard. Be very careful in doing this. Perhaps the easiest way for you to cut off excess tape is to do so in four different parts.

   First, you may cut off the excess tape on the two flat sides. After doing so, you may cut off excess tape on the two round sides, along the tail and nose of your skateboard.

5. Grab the pencil or whatever object you've chosen to poke the board holes with. Poke the eight holes of your skateboard through the grip tape you just attached.

This should make it a lot easier for you to attach the hardware to your board and make the process a lot quicker as well. In fact, this technique is used by a lot of skateboarders, regardless of whether they're beginners or masters in the sport.

So, that's it!

Gripping your skateboard isn't really a very complicated process, although it can take a bit of getting used to and there's a chance you'll make a mistake the first time around.

The good thing is that it's easy enough to make adjustments to correct mistakes in applying grip tape to your board.

There's really no need for you to go to a skateboarding shop just to have the grip attached or to bother an experienced skateboarder about the task. It's an easy enough DIY project.

Besides, gripping your own board can be quite fulfilling. And once it's done, you can put the board onto the trucks and start enjoying the sport.

Essential Tips for Beginners

Just like any other sport, you'll need to practice your skills daily and master the basics if you want to do well in skateboarding.

In fact, whether your ultimate goal is to become known as one of the world's skateboarding masters or the sport is simply a hobby you enjoy doing from time to time, the basics is where you need to start.

The best in any sport, after all, never gives up on practicing and mastering the basics.

Here are some basic tips for beginners in the sport of skateboarding:

1. Identify Your Dominant Foot

When you skateboard, your dominant foot is normally positioned on your board's tail end. That's because the dominant foot does the steering. This foot is usually the one that leads when you walk.

Observe yourself as you walk up the stairs. The foot that takes the first step is likely to be your dominant foot. When you skate with your left foot forward, you have what's generally known as a regular stance.

But, if you skate with your right foot forward, your stance is generally known as a goofy stance.

When you skate with your feet positioned in the opposite of your normal stance, then you're said to be "riding switch."

2. Find the Best Practice Location

The best place for you to practice skateboarding is an area where there's a great deal of level turf and where you'll have a lot of room in which to move.

You may also want to look for an area where there are a few hills or grade, like a driveway. It would be best, though, if the hills and grades don't lead directly onto a street where passing cars could possibly hit you. An empty parking lot may be your best option.

3. Watch Videos

If you plan to invest in skateboarding lessons, then it may be a good idea for you to watch some online videos first.

There are plenty of videos that demonstrate how to execute skateboarding tricks and moves, from the most basic to the most complicated.

When you watch these videos, be sure to focus on the skateboarder's legs, then way they position their feet on the board, and the degree to which they bend their knees.

There are also some skateboarding moves that require you to bend your knees at just the right time, so you'll have to take note of those moves and their timing as well.

Try executing the moves a few times, so when you finally take lessons, you'll already be aware of where you usually have problems. This also lets you know the right questions to ask.

Knowing your strengths and weaknesses beforehand also helps you choose the right instructor.

Remember to take the task of learning how to skateboard one day at a time. Focus on the basics and don't be too excited to try fancy tricks immediately.

You should also refrain from trying to execute dangerous stunts too soon.

Be patient and you'll surely be able to enjoy the best of the sport.

Riding a Skateboard

As soon as you've determined your skateboarding stance, you should be ready to start riding.

And the first thing you need to learn when you ride is how to push on your board. In order to push successfully, you need to place one foot by the board's nose and then keep it there at all times.

It is best to position your foot on top of the board's front hardware so you won't have to move it to make room for the other foot after pushing.

The foot you use to push off will be the one positioned on the back part of the board.

Try to keep this foot close to your skateboard's side. You're likely to lose your balance if this foot is positioned too far from the board.

Once you learn how to push off properly, you'll also have to learn how to get onto the board without automatically falling off.

The most basic way of getting on, of course, is to simply place your pushing foot behind the other after you push.

Another way to get on is by jogging a bit and then hopping onto the board with a wide stance and your knees slightly bent to absorb your landing.

You could also try starting off by holding your board's nose in one hand with your arm extended such that the board is held in front of you.

Place your front foot over the front hardware while dropping the board to the ground and then immediately place your back foot over the back hardware as you start to roll.

Once you get rolling, you'll have to learn how to turn as well. There are basically two ways for you to turn on your skateboard. The first is simply by leaning your weight onto one side of the board.

Take note that the more you lean, the sharper your turn will be. If your trucks aren't too tight, then you'll need less pressure to turn.

The second way to turn is by pressing the board's tail with your back foot and then guiding your front foot towards your desired direction.

It's best to position your front foot over the front hardware when doing this.

Learning how to stop is just as important as learning how to push off when you skateboard.

One effective way of stopping a skateboard is by taking your back foot off the board and then slowly dragging it on the ground. When you do so, be sure to drag your foot towards the front of the board to avoid tripping.

Another option is for you to simply apply pressure to the board's tail so as to scrape it on the ground. The more pressure you apply, the quicker you will stop.

The most fun way to stop is by swinging your skateboard's back wheels 90 degrees. This will have you sliding with all wheels faced forward, which causes you to gradually lose speed until you stop completely.

Now, are you wondering if there are special ways of getting of your skateboard as well?

There may be, but once you start learning how to ride, you'll probably have so much fun that you wouldn't want to get off.

Tricks for Beginners

Among the things that make skateboarding so attractive are the various tricks and stunts that skateboarders do.

Although these tricks can be very difficult to learn and are a bit risky, you can execute them in a perfectly safe manner by wearing the necessary protective gear.

In skateboarding competitions, these tricks and stunts are among the most important factors that judges consider when weighing the performances of participants.

Judgement in this case is based on such parameters as creativity, difficulty level, and ease of performance.

And while these tricks can indeed be difficult to master, they're not really impossible for you to learn, even as a beginner.

Here are a few skateboarding tricks you may want to start out with:

1. 50-50 Grind

This trick involves sliding along a bench or railing. You may start practicing this trick with a ledge and just move on to using a rail when you've mastered it.

To achieve high speed as you come onto the ledge, it's best to start from a good distance.

Be sure to position your feet in the same way you would when doing the Ollie as you move towards the ledge.

Ollie right onto the ledge in such a way that it stays in the middle after you bend your knees upon approaching the ledge.

It helps to bend forward a bit so as to maintain balance. Lift your board and then jump when you reach the edge to make sure you land on the board's wheels.

2. Board Sliding

This trick involves jumping onto a rail and then sliding along it before landing perfectly back on the ground.

You'll have to make sure the rail onto which you slide is waxed adequately for this trick so you'll have a smooth ride.

As you move towards the rail, position your feet the way you would when doing the Ollie. The rail should be behind your heels as you ride.

After you do the Ollie, turn at a right angle so the rail remains in the middle of the skateboard and bend your knees to maintain balance.

As you jump off the rail, turn at a right angle towards the opposite direction.

3. Caveman

This trick is among the very first skateboarding tricks you should learn, although you should start learning it only when you've had a bit of experience riding your board.

You begin the trick by standing on the ground with your board held in one hand.

Be sure to hold your skateboard with your fingers and then place your thumb on the grip.

Swing your skateboard such that you hold it on the nose end and allow the tail end to swing away from you. As it swings back towards you, jump onto the skateboard as you release it and it falls to the ground.

These are just three of the simpler tricks you can start learning as a beginner in the sport of skateboarding.

As your skills improve and you become more confident in your skateboarding abilities, you can start learning more complicated moves as well.

What's most important is that you stay safe while doing so.

Improving Your Skateboarding Style

Style is very important in skateboarding compctitions.

You can master as many skateboarding tricks as you want, but unless you're able to develop your own style, then you probably would never be counted among the world's greatest skateboarders.

If you're experiencing some issues with improving your skateboarding style or you simply don't know where and how to start doing so, then you could definitely use the tips in this article.

The first thing you should do, of course, is determine what style you'll be using.

It would help for you to watch some videos to see what the different skateboarding styles are.

Try out different styles to see which one feels most comfortable.

Now, you should be ready to make the most out of the sport.

1. Be Comfortable

Before you can ever hope to improve your skateboarding style, you have to be comfortable with the act of skateboarding.

This means you should have practiced to such extent that you can move comfortably as one with your board.

Towards this end, you should make sure you're using the type of board that's best suited to the type of skater that you are.

You may want to seek advice from a skateboarding expert to find the right board or perhaps you'd rather try different types of board to determine which feels most comfortable.

Once you find the right board type, make the necessary adjustments to truly make it your own.

Most importantly, you should be able to gain full control of your skateboard.

2. Be In Control

As mentioned earlier, gaining full control of your skateboard is essential for improving your skateboarding style.

Among other things, you'll have to gain the ability to control the way your skateboard moves even as you execute a high trick.

If you lose control of your board at any point, then you'll likely wobble around struggling to regain control.

When this happens, style will most probably be the last thing you think about.

Remember as well that good balance is crucial to having full control of the board.

To achieve balance, you'll have to lean towards different directions from time to time to keep from falling flat on the ground.

If you feel yourself starting to fall forwards, lean back until you regain balance.

It's also a good idea to bend your knees when you execute tricks, as this also helps you maintain balance.

3. Master Your Technique

Before you show off a new skateboarding trick you've learned, be sure to master it first.

Although there will still be times when you'll mess up, even when your skateboarding skills have improved significantly, you should have the ability to execute your tricks perfectly most of the time.

This is the only way you can ever hope to do those tricks with style. The best way to enhance your skills and master your tricks is, of course, to keep practicing.

As long as you keep these tips in mind, you should be on your way towards improving your skateboarding style and maybe even winning your first few competitions.

Mastering Tricks

There are several different skateboarding tricks you'll have to learn if you really want to become known in this sport.

The problem is that you could feel a bit overwhelmed by the amount of tips you're likely to get as regards learning these tricks.

There's a set of tips for every single trick to learn and videos that show you how to execute the trick.

As a beginner, however, you may want to get some general tips on executing skateboarding tricks properly without going into the details of each trick.

You may already have been skateboarding for a while and perhaps you already know a number of tricks as well as some techniques on building on those tricks, but you may still feel the need to work on mastering these tricks.

Perhaps you've learned the basics and wish to proceed to more advanced moves, but you're not quite that confident about your skills to really believe you can pull it off.

Whatever your current skill level is, the following tips will surely help you master whatever skateboarding trick you're interested in.

1. Body Positioning and Stance

Your stance and the manner in which your body is positioned matter a lot in mastering skateboarding tricks.

In fact, these two factors are crucial to the completion of certain tricks.

When you practice each trick, it's advisable to observe how your board and your body are positioned as you land.

You may want to do the trick in different directions so you'll see how the change in direction affects your body positioning.

Just like almost anything else in life, practice is the key to getting your body positioning and stance right when performing skateboarding tricks.

2. Shoulder Alignment

When you perform skateboarding tricks, you should also make sure your shoulders are properly aligned.

Remember that every person performs tricks in a different way, so it can be a bit difficult to say for sure where your shoulders have to be for any given trick.

The general idea, however, is to be aware of your normal skateboarding style and then take note of where you instinctively position your shoulders whenever you successfully perform a trick.

The next time you execute that trick, try to position your shoulders in the same exact way.

When you get used to this manner of doing the trick, your movements and shoulder placement should already come naturally.

You may also want to watch videos of people executing the tricks you want to learn so you can see how they line their shoulders up.

There are several different movements of your body that has to be considered when you perform skateboarding tricks.

The above tips are just some general guidelines you can keep in mind to begin with.

Once you've mastered these basics and they've become second nature to you, you can start exploring more advanced tricks and making use of techniques that are specific to whatever trick you want to master.

The beauty of skateboarding is that there's always something new for you to learn, thus keeping things interesting.

32011622R00060

Made in the USA
Middletown, DE
04 January 2019